W9-BEX-988

Skipper's Practical Handbook

Skipper's Practical Handbook

RICHARD CROOKS

John Wiley & Sons, Ltd

Published under the Fernhurst imprint by John Wiley & Sons Ltd, The Atrium, Southern Gate, Chichester, West Sussex PO19 8SQ, England

Telephone   (+44) 1243 779777

Email (for orders and customer service enquiries): cs-books@wiley.co.uk
Visit our Home Page on www.wiley.com

Other Wiley Editorial Offices

John Wiley & Sons Inc., 111 River Street, Hoboken, NJ 07030, USA

Jossey-Bass, 989 Market Street, San Francisco, CA 94103-1741, USA

Wiley-VCH Verlag GmbH, Boschstr. 12, D-69469 Weinheim, Germany

John Wiley & Sons Australia Ltd, 42 McDougall Street, Milton, Queensland 4064, Australia

John Wiley & Sons (Asia) Pte Ltd, 2 Clementi Loop #02-01, Jin Xing Distripark, Singapore 129809

John Wiley & Sons Canada Ltd, 6045 Freemont Blvd. Mississauga, Ontario, L5R 4J3, Canada

Wiley also publishes its books in a variety of electronic formats. Some content that appears in print may not be available in electronic books.

Library of Congress Cataloging-in-Publication Data.

Crooks, R.C.
  Skipper's practical handbook / R.C. Crooks.
     p. cm.
  Includes bibliographical references and index.
  ISBN-13: 978-0-470-05971-5 (pbk. : alk. paper)
  ISBN-10: 0-470-05971-0 (pbk. : alk. paper)
  1. Boats and boating–Handbooks, manuals, etc. I. Title.
  GV775.C76'2007
  797.1–dc22

                        2006026718

British Library Cataloguing in Publication Data

A catalogue record for this book is available from the British Library

ISBN-13: 978-0-470-05971-5 (PB)
ISBN-10: 0-470-05971-0 (PB)

Typeset in 9/12 Swiss 721 by Laserwords Private Limited, Chennai, India
Printed in China through World Print, Hong Kong
This book is printed on acid-free paper responsibly manufactured from sustainable forestry
in which at least two trees are planted for each one used for paper production.

Contents

Preface

One of the many reasons I love sailing is that it provides a constant learning opportunity. Every time I am on the water I learn something new and look forward to the next cruise or race with a mixture of excitement and healthy apprehension. There are so many variables that a skipper can never take success for granted. The combination of yacht characteristics, crew, weather, wind and tide always provides a situation requiring some thought.

This complexity provides a daunting challenge for any practical book on sailing and possibly explains why there are so few in relation to the numerous volumes on sailing theory. Neither is there a real substitute for experience and a skipper's mental database of things that worked well and those that didn't grows during every trip.

Nevertheless, for any skipper to avoid similar mistakes or to repeat successes it is vital to understand why they happened: 'Why did my bow hit the pontoon?' or 'Why was my crew unable to pick up that mooring buoy?' The first aim of this book, therefore, is to help the skipper understand why a yacht behaves the way it does[1].

---

[1] To reduce some variability, I have assumed that your yacht is a fin keel Bermudan sloop with an aft cockpit, simply because

On every passage a skipper will have to deal with several practical challenges. Some will occur frequently, such as powering into a tight marina berth in strong wind and others hopefully less often, such as sailing onto an anchorage because the engine cannot be started. Like life, any complex problem can be solved by breaking it down into simpler, constituent parts. So the second aim is to present the skipper with a tool box: a series of sequential steps that can be learned and used to solve all the common power handling, sailing and navigational scenarios. In my experience teaching as an RYA Yachtmaster Instructor, knowledge breeds confidence, which in turn fosters enjoyment.

Personally, I get great satisfaction from getting from A to B without the engine if that's possible. If I can sail off the pontoon, out of the river and then onto a mooring buoy in time for lunch, I will have had a great morning. And you never know when you may actually be forced to do so in an emergency. So if this book encourages you to practice, learn and enjoy, then its final aim will have been met.

Happy sailing.

Richard Crooks

---

these form the vast majority of yachts bought and chartered today.

Introduction

The *Skipper's Practical Handbook* is a companion to the popular *Skipper's Pocketbook*. The latter is a handy aide-memoir of much of the data that a skipper needs to know and covers the content of a typical shore-based sailing course. The *Skipper's Practical Handbook*, however, assumes the skipper already possesses that theoretical knowledge and is designed as an aide-memoir for practising the more advanced practical aspects of yacht handling. Sailing instructors may find this book a useful reference.

The book does not cover the basic practical crew work. There are many other excellent books covering that subject. The assumption is that the skipper has onboard a competent crew.

Clearly, there is always more than one way to achieve a successful outcome. Many skippers will have learned or been taught successful techniques different to those covered here. Further, the yacht you are sailing may have quite different handling characteristics from the common fin-keel Bermudan sloop used as the reference boat. However, the techniques in this book simply represent those that, as an instructor, I have found to be: a) simple to explain; b) repeatable and c) ultimately the most successful.

Section 1 – Safety Brief. This is comprehensive check-list to help a skipper remember all aspects of safety that should be explained before every passage.

Section 2 – Skippering Style. No matter how technically competent the skipper, sailing is a team sport and leveraging the skills within the team is key to success and enjoyment. This section contains a few ideas to avoid the common pitfalls that characterise a poor team leader.

Section 3 – Power Handling. Let's be honest, sailing is the easy bit. The difficult part occurs leaving or arriving at the berth under power. There will be tide and wind and an exciting profusion of expensive yachts nearby. As a flotilla skipper in Greece, I found that some pre-emptive coaching tended to reduce the excitement at these daily events. This section starts by explaining the six principles of power handling: 1) windage; 2) prop kick or walk; 3) prop wash; 4) pivot point; 5) slide and 6) minimum operating speed. The section then describes various common scenarios for the skipper to solve using knowledge of these principles. The skipper should always make space and time to think through the problem. Always have a plan of action and a contingency if the original plan fails.

Section 4 – Handling Under Sail. Any skipper can hoist the canvass and sail the yacht in the general right direction. But even the most casual cruising skipper must get slightly irritated when a similar yacht overtakes to claim the last berth or the last order. This section starts with an explanation of the three main principles of sailing fast and efficiently: 1) sail shape; 2) sail twist; 3) sail balance. The section then describes how to trim the sails to create the optimum shape, twist and balance depending on the wind strength and sea state. This should be basic revision and there are numerous weighty and excellent volumes on this topic. The section then describes various common sailing manoeuvres for the skipper to solve.

Section 5 – Man Over Board. When was the last time you practised your MOB drill? Could your crew come and rescue you if you were careless or unlucky enough to fall in? Remember that the view of the coroner dictates that MOB is a power handling exercise not a sailing exercise (unless there is a very good reason why the engine could not be started.) Next time you sail, why not practice the drill explained in this section. It works.

Section 6 – Navigation. This section assumes the skipper possesses a good knowledge of shore-based theory and there are many excellent books covering that subject. Most skippers try to plan their trips in advance. But life conspires against even the well organised skipper: the wind is in a different quarter (that nice reach that was forecast has turned into a beat) or the crew have turned up two hours late. The skipper must then be able to solve a slightly different problem and rather more quickly. In an exam situation, it is unusual for the skipper to have much more than 30 minutes to plan a two hour passage. This section starts by focusing on a real passage. It contains some techniques for using onboard to: a) speed up the navigation planning and b) ensure the passage sailed is the most efficient. The section then describes practical techniques for navigating without GPS or radar in poor visibility, i.e. fog or at night.

Section 7 – Passage Planning. This section presents a simple checklist of steps a skipper should perform on any offshore passage. It presents a real passage explaining each step in turn. Neither passage planning nor navigation can always be performed in the comfort of home or classroom and without time constraints. Techniques are described to help speed up the process. Included are interpolations designed for speed that may reduce the accuracy of the numbers. The skipper must judge in every scenario what margin of error is acceptable. Ultimately, speed comes with practise and good judgement through experience.

I hope you enjoy the book and that it becomes a well-thumbed volume as you practice getting more out of your sailing.

Picture Credits

All Hydrographic Office charts used in this book are © Crown Copyright and/or database rights. Reproduced by permission of the Controller of Her Majesty's Stationery Office and the UK Hydrographic Office (www. ukho.gov.uk)

Imray Chart C12 is copyright © Crown Copyright and/or database rights. Reproduced by permission of the Controller of Her Majesty's Stationery Office and the UK Hydrographic Office (www.ukho.gov.uk), and Imray Laurie Norie and Wilson, Ltd.

Safety Brief

Best practice demands that before any journey, all items related to safety are checked. Below are two safety brief checklists; one covering below decks, the second, above deck.

Down Below

1. MOB
   - Lifejackets
   - Safety lines

2. Fire
   - Gas stop valve & procedure
   - Gas alarm & procedure
   - Fire extinguishers & procedure
   - Fuel shut off
   - Fire blanket

3. Flooding
   - Sea cocks and bungs
   - Electric bilge pump

4. Distress Signals
   - VHF
   - DSC
   - Emergency antennae
   - EPIRB

5. Restricted Visibility
    - Fog horns
    - Torches and searchlight
6. First Aid
    - Normal first aid box
    - Category C first aid box

Topsides

1. MOB
    - Strong points e.g. D-rings, jackstays
    - Horseshoe buoys. Danbuoy
    - Recovery (heaving line, Jonbuoy etc.)
2. Fire
    - Gas bottle
    - Engine fire extinguisher and procedure
3. Flooding
    - Manual bilge pumps
    - Hand pumps and buckets
4. Distress Signals
    - Hand held VHF
    - Flares (parachute and red hand held)
    - Orange smoke
5. Restricted Visibility
    - Radar reflector
    - White hand held flare
6. Abandon Ship
    - Life raft
    - Grab bag
7. Miscellaneous
    - Draft and depth gauge calibration
    - Storm jib and trisail
    - Kedge anchor
    - Emergency tiller and operation
    - Bolt croppers

Skippering Style

A s skipper, best practice requires that you ensure the following at all times:

- make sure you are always in control

- make sure all crew members are kept busy

- make sure all crew members are clear about what everyone is doing

- make sure everyone on board is enjoying themselves

DELEGATION

Whatever the size of your crew, make sure you use everyone. It's not uncommon to find skippers who are used to short-handed sailing running around cleating off lines on the bow, while crew members sit idly by watching, probably bored.

Remember, if your head is down over a cleat, are you in a good position to see potential problems? When managing manoeuvres, you should be at or near the helm and throttle control. This will allow you to
- see the 'big picture'

- control the boat quickly should some crew work not go as planned

Make sure you delegate tasks sensibly. For example, it's wise to have your best lassoer on the bow when sailing onto a mooring buoy; however, try not to exclude anyone.

CLEAR COMMUNICATION

As in life, poor communication is a recipe for confusion and failure. The following three tips will help with effective communication:

1. Make sure everybody uses the same language: Your crew may have come from diverse sailing backgrounds and may use slightly different jargon for the same jobs. For example, crews use many different terms for 'easing' (to pay out) or 'slipping' (to release and bring onboard) lines. Ensure you all understand and use the same terms.

2. Make sure you are specific: Common requests heard on yachts include: 'Will someone…' or 'Can we…'. This lack of precision has one of two effects – either everyone rushes to do the same job or no one does.

3. Make sure you are heard: This is common sense but worth emphasising, especially if it's very windy. Ensure the crew all look at each other when speaking and raise their voices appropriately so as to be heard. Sometimes, it's worth having a crew member relaying messages from bow to stern (or even from helm to navigation table, when navigating 'blind'). It's a good idea to rehearse and agree your communication techniques before a trip.

RUNNING A HAPPY BOAT

All sailors want an enjoyable time on board and this is one of your main responsibilities as skipper. The following tips may help, especially when sailing with strangers:

1. Make a domestic work rota like the one in the table below. Avoid disagreements over the housekeeping by dividing tasks among all the crew (including yourself of course) before the passage.

Task	Mon	Tue	Wed	Thu	Fri
Breakfast	Crew A	Crew B	Crew C	Crew D	Crew A
Lunch	Crew B	Crew C	Crew D	Crew A	Crew B
Supper	Crew C	Crew D	Crew A	Crew B	Crew C
Clean heads	Crew D	Crew A	Crew B	Crew C	Crew D
Prepare topsides	Crew A	Crew B	Crew C	Crew D	Crew A
Get weather	Crew B	Crew C	Crew D	Crew A	Crew B
Check engine	Crew C	Crew D	Crew A	Crew B	Crew C

2. Be assertive, but not aggressive: Ask nicely, and if a crew member ever misunderstands you, don't assume it's his or her fault. Ask yourself whether you communicated what you wanted clearly enough? Be patient and try again – shouting the same instructions louder won't have the desired effect.

3. Be honest: It's unlikely everything on a trip will go quite to plan. But as skipper the buck stops with you. For example, if you're approaching a mooring buoy too fast, bail out and try again. You can't blame your crew for failing to lasso a buoy at 2 knots over the ground!

4. Have a laugh: Take it seriously, of course, but see the funny side when appropriate.

Power Handling

B est practice requires that all skippers should be able to handle a yacht under power in close-quarters. This chapter contains some exercises, scenarios and games for you to practise the art of power handling.

WINDAGE EXERCISE

Assuming there is some wind, go out into a clear area of the marina or river, preferably out of the tide. Stop the yacht, centre the helm and see what happens.

Notice how the bow is lighter and has less underwater surface resistance than the stern. Remember that on a fin keel yacht, the quarter seeks the wind.

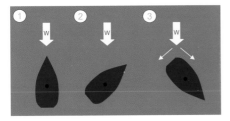

PROP KICK OR WALK EXERCISE

Once the yacht is sitting stably to the wind, keep the helm centred and apply a long burst of astern, while looking back at the bow. Notice which way the bow moves. Propellers are either clockwise or anticlockwise screws and have a paddle-wheel effect that 'walks' or 'kicks' the stern either to port or starboard. This can happen to a negligible, small or large degree depending on the yacht.

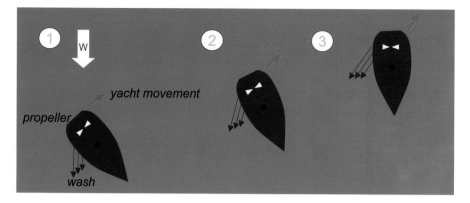

In the above figure, the yacht 'kicks to port' in astern initially. As the yacht gathers speed, the water running over the centred rudder tends to straighten the movement of the yacht as it moves astern. Remember to 'dip the bow' to port before going astern in this yacht, as the prop kick will naturally straighten the yacht.

PROP WASH EXERCISE

Stop the yacht again in plenty of room. Put the helm hard over to one side so that the rudder is at its maximum deflecting angle. Apply a lengthy burst of forward gear. The wash from the propeller hits the rudder at its maximum angle and bounces off. The equal and opposite reaction to this moves the stern the opposite way, spinning the yacht around.

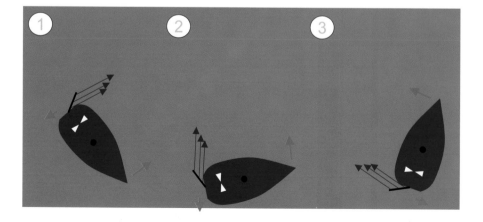

In the previous page figure, we have put our wheel hard over to port. Remember: 'Stop/Steer/Go' – get the helm over hard before applying power, so that most prop wash is turned into turning effort and very little into forward momentum.

PIVOT POINT EXERCISE

When doing the prop wash exercise, did you notice how the yacht seemed to spin around its centre somewhere near the mast? In forward gear the pivot point of a fin keel yacht is near the keel/mast. Stop the yacht again, 'dip the bow' and motor astern until the yacht is heading straight backwards and responding to the wheel. Turn hard first one way and then the other. Always keep holding onto the wheel to avoid it snatching. Watch the bow at all times.

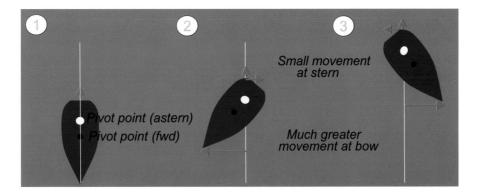

Notice how the stern seems to move only a few feet sideways, whereas the bow slews around to a much greater extent. Remember: In astern, the pivot point of a yacht moves aft (towards the centre of the cockpit). So keep one eye on your bow at all times.

SLIDE EXERCISE

Motor forwards at a few knots if there is enough room. Put the helm hard over to one side. Look at the yacht's wake over your shoulder after the turn. Its motion is not like a train on rails, but more like a rally car skidding or 'sliding' around a gravelly bend. The momentum of the yacht carries the yacht forwards while the rudder turns the yacht to one side.

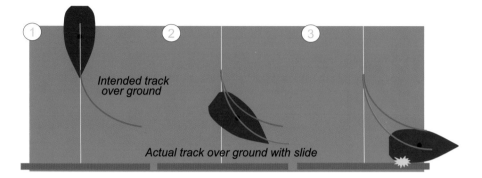

Intended track over ground

Actual track over ground with slide

This 'slide' is easier to demonstrate near a fixed point such as a pontoon. Remember: To reduce slide in a turn, ensure you have minimum entry speed. Slide can also be used to your advantage (as we will see later).

MINIMUM OPERATING SPEED (MOS) EXERCISE

Minimum Operating Speed (MOS) is the slowest yacht speed you need to keep control of the yacht, i.e. to maintain steerage. Steerage is caused by water flowing over the rudder. The more flow, the more steerage. In no tide, the yacht motoring or sailing through the water causes this flow. In example 3 in the figure below, there is no steerage despite motoring through the water at 2 knots in the same direction as the tide.

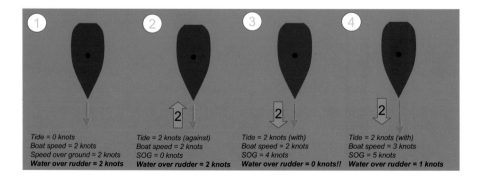

Tide = 0 knots	Tide = 2 knots (against)	Tide = 2 knots (with)	Tide = 2 knots (with)
Boat speed = 2 knots	Boat speed = 2 knots	Boat speed = 2 knots	Boat speed = 3 knots
Speed over ground = 2 knots	SOG = 0 knots	SOG = 4 knots	SOG = 5 knots
Water over rudder = 2 knots	**Water over rudder = 2 knots**	**Water over rudder = 0 knots!!**	**Water over rudder = 1 knots**

We have to 'overtake' the tide (see example 4 in the figure) in order to get net water flowing over the rudder! If the yacht is stationary over the ground in a flowing tide, (e.g. tied to a pontoon or mooring buoy, at anchor) the tide flowing over the rudder will give steerage.

Note that example 2 in the figure is called 'stemming the tide' and is the principle used in 'ferry gliding'.

TURNING IN A CONFINED SPACE

Let's have a look at turning in a confined space. Once you have determined which way the prop kicks, execute a power turn in an open area: stop the boat to reduce slide; turn the helm hard over (stop/steer/go); apply short heavy burst of forwards (prop wash) and then astern (prop walk reverse); don't move the helm throughout the manoeuvre; try and keep the boat turning within its own length and not drifting down with any tide or leeway.

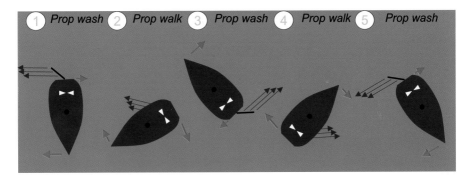

If your boat kicks to port, which way will you have the helm, to starboard or to port? In the figure above, we have a no tide, no wind, power turn. Our boat kicks to port so we execute the prop wash with our wheel hard to starboard.

Scenario A

Now, let's make things more interesting! Find a lane between pontoons of finger berths in a marina. Plan to go in and make a power turn. This is a common scenario if you need to check out a berth given to you by a harbour master. What is the tide doing? What is the wind doing? Are you confident enough to turn without scratching the boat?

In the example in the figure on the right, we have no wind, but there is a 2 knot spring tide flowing out of the river. The tide slackens as we get into shallower water nearer the shore. Our prop kicks to port. What do you do?

Scenario A: Solution

See the figure below for the solution to Scenario A.

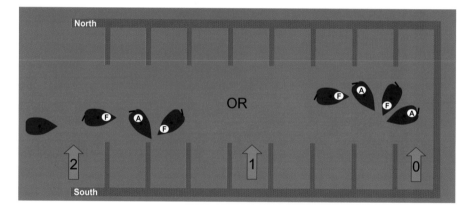

Here are a few tips to help:

- Which is the stronger element – wind or tide? Always turn into the tide if that is the stronger. Here you turn to starboard, so we can also use prop walk to help us.

- More tide over our rudder will help us steer around.

- The tide will set you down onto the North boats. Keep as up-tide as possible. You can reduce the tide by going shallower, but this also reduces the steerage you get from the tide.

- The pivot point will kick your stern out to port on your initial prop wash turn. Give yourself enough room from the boats in the North.

Scenario B

In this scenario, we have no tide. However, a good Force 6 breeze is blowing from the North.

You could try a prop walk turn to starboard. The breeze will certainly help blow your bow off to starboard in the beginning.

But what happens when you are halfway through the turn? How will you get the bow around against the wind when you are almost stationary?

Scenario B: Solution

See the figure below for the solution to Scenario B.

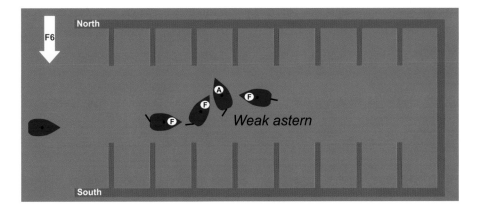

Here are some tips to help:

- Wind is the stronger element here; so strong that you'll have to turn through it using prop wash.

- Once the bow is through the wind, the wind completes the turn for you!

- If you have to use astern, do it gently so as to minimise prop walk, which will counter your turn in this instance.

- Remember to keep that minimum operating speed so that you can steer to keep the bow against the wind as you motor in.

Scenario C

In this scenario, we have both wind and tide. Which is the stronger? Do we turn through the tide or turn through the wind?

There is no right or wrong answer here. It's fun working out what is going off now in your immediate vicinity. All you need is a simple plan that is most likely to be executed safely.

Scenario C: Solution

See the figure below for the solution to Scenario C.

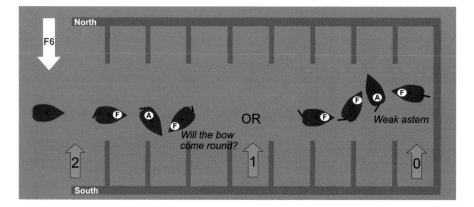

You could execute a prop walk turn in the strong tide and hope this gives you enough steerage to get the bow pointing back out into the river. Conversely, you could negate the tide by going into the shallows and turning through the wind.

A good tip is always to look for tell tale signs of the strength of the tide, e.g. to what extent are you having to 'crab' sideways to counter the tide?

Also, check if there is any lee, e.g. behind a large powerboat, which might negate any troublesome windage?

POWER TURN GAME

Here's a game for you to try. Get a whiteboard and a dry wipe marker and create the template below. Use this to alter wind and tide direction and strength to create some challenging scenarios. Have fun!

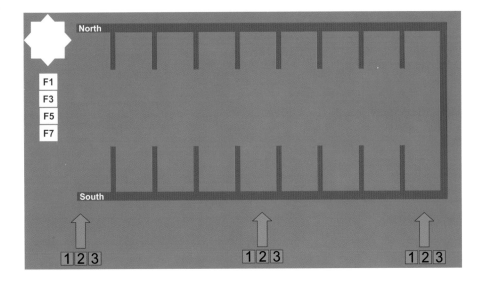

COMING ALONGSIDE

Best practice demands that you know how to park the boat alongside a pontoon at the end of a journey.

The following scenarios will allow you to practise the following:

- Tide awareness

- Wind awareness

- Boat handling skills

- Skippering ability, i.e. crew management and communication skills

Don't forget the basics:
- What is the tide doing and how strong is it?

- What is the wind strength? Is it blowing me onto the pontoon, off the pontoon or neither?

Remember always to approach into any significant tide. This will give you both brakes and steerage at low speed over the ground.

I've assumed that you can remember to ensure your yacht is appropriately fendered at all times and to tie it up properly! But remember to brief your crew before-hand about what you want to happen and when.

Scenario A: No Wind

In this scenario (see figure on the right) we have no significant wind, maybe a F2 blowing off the pontoon. There is a strong spring tide flooding up the river. Your task is to come alongside safely.

Scenario A: Solution

See the figure below for the solution to Scenario A.

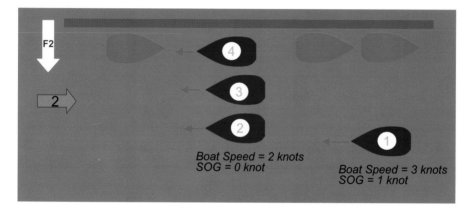

This scenario allows you to practise your 'ferry gliding' technique. Simply pull alongside the space and meas-ure up. Then 'stem the tide', i.e. make your SOG zero.

Turn the helm to starboard and steer into the pontoon; then straighten up. Repeat until your fenders gently nudge the pontoon.

Scenario B: Wind On

In this scenario (see figure on the right), we have a sig-nificant wind blowing us onto the pontoon.

We have some tide, but it's not strong enough to use your 'ferry gliding' skills without losing the bow to the stronger wind. However, the space you have is a little bigger.

The task is to come alongside safely and then get your yacht out again to continue your passage.

A good rule of thumb to remember is that 1 knot of tide is equivalent in effect to 15 knots of wind on the yacht.

Scenario B: Solution

See the figure below for the solution to Scenario B.

Boat Speed = 1 knots
SOG = 0.5 knot

For a wind-on pontoon, the approach angle can be shallow. Here are some tips:

- Ensure any tide and leeway doesn't set you down onto the parked boat. Line up a point on your yacht (e.g. a shroud) with a point on the pontoon (e.g. a cleat) and motor down that transit.

- Maintain the MOS to stop your bow being taken into the pontoon.

- Try not to use bursts of astern, as the prop walk will kick your stern away from the pontoon.

- The stern breast line is the more important to get tied up first and tight. This will prevent the bow being blown into the pontoon. The more important spring is the stern spring.

To leave a wind-on pontoon, you have to power against a spring line (see figure on page 18).

Bow spring rigged as a slip

You could motor astern against a stern spring: the tide will help swing the bow out. However, the wind will try to blow the bow back in. Alternatively, you could motor forward against a bow spring because the wind is not working against you. However, be aware that the tide will try and push the stern back in, although not by much.

A bow spring will pivot the stern out a longer way (than a stern spring pivots the bow out) because of the shape of a yacht. Your prop walk to port will also help here.

Ensure you have a steep enough angle to clear parked boats before slipping.

Scenario C: Wind Off

In this scenario (see figure on the right), we have an even more significant wind blowing us off the pontoon.

The task is to come alongside safely and then get your yacht out again to continue your passage. How do you get close to the pontoon with the wind blowing your bow away?

Scenario C: Solution

See the figure below for the solution to Scenario C.

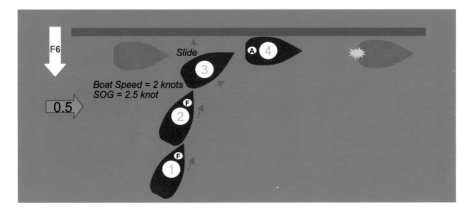

For a wind-off pontoon, the approach angle must be steeper and the approach bolder. Here are some tips:

- Keep the SOG higher and turn away a little earlier, using slide to carry the boat alongside.

- As your approach speed is higher, you must use more astern to stop the boat. A port side approach will ensure your stern is kicked into and not away from the pontoon.

- Your bow breast line must be attached quickly to prevent the bow being blown off.

To leave a wind-off pontoon, simply ease the bow breast line first and let the wind do the rest (see the following figure).

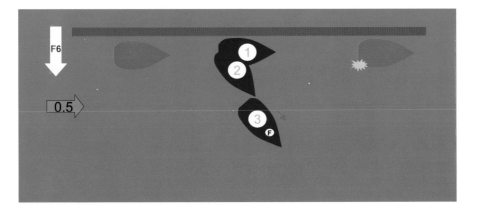

If the tide is more significant than the wind, ensure you use the tide to help you drift out. In this scenario, if the tide was 2 knots, ease the stern breast line first. The tide will swing the yacht out. Then motor out astern.

ALONGSIDE GAME 1

Here are a couple more games to try. Get a whiteboard and a dry wipe marker and create the template on the right. Use this to alter wind and tide direction and strength to create some challenging scenarios.

ALONGSIDE GAME 2

Again, get a whiteboard and a dry wipe marker and create the following template. Use this to alter wind and tide direction and strength. Attempting to park in bays A through D will test your skills. Don't be afraid to think laterally or be ingenious. There's no wrong way as long as it works and is safe. Have fun!

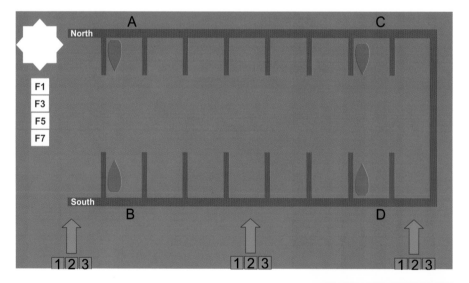

SINGLE LINE MOORING

Let's return to Scenario C on page 18 (coming alongside safely, with a significant wind blowing us off the pontoon and no significant tide).

How do you get close to the pontoon with the wind blowing your bow away? How can you get your crew safely on the pontoon without them having to jump and take risks? What would you do if you are sailing short-handed and no one is around to help take your lines?

The following figure shows three options. In all three cases:

- Rig a mooring line of appropriate length as a lasso and throw it over an appropriate cleat as you motor by without the crew stepping ashore.

- Motor forward gently against the line trying not to snatch the bow into the pontoon. Solution 3 helps avoid this.

- Put the helm over to starboard and throttle forward to pin the stern of the yacht into the pontoon. You'll have to keep adjusting helm and throttle until you get the appropriate balance.

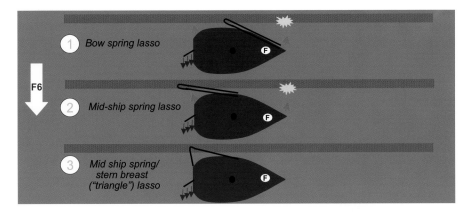

Pile Mooring

Pile moorings are found in tidal rivers, especially in the Solent (e.g. Cowes, Yarmouth, Lymington, Beaulieu and the River Itchen). They are normally aligned with the flow of the stream.

Pile moorings provide a good all round test of best practice when handling a yacht under power.

As with all other manoeuvres – but especially with pile moorings – proper planning and preparation are key to a successful execution.

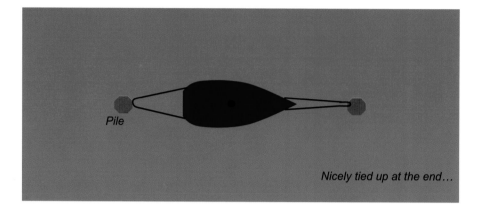

Pile

Nicely tied up at the end...

Pile Mooring: Preparation

The first stage in pile mooring is preparation. Look at the figure below.

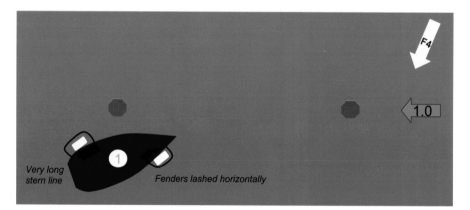

Very long stern line   *Fenders lashed horizontally*

1 You need to ask yourself what the tide and wind are doing? Always perform a 'drive by' of the piles to confirm your knowledge of these elements and then start formulating your plan.

You must aim to:
• approach into any significant tide;

- pass leeward of the down tide pile to attach your stern lines;

- rest windward of the up-tide pile to attach your bow line.

Also, bear in mind the following tips:
- Be properly fendered on your stern quarter and bow. Piles can be hard metal and rusty!

- Ensure your mooring lines are long enough. The stern slip must be nearly twice the distance between the piles!

Pile Mooring: The Stern Line

You now need to attach the stern line (see the following figure).

2. Have your long stern line flaked out nicely on the port quarter. Motor gently downwind of the first pile, trying to keep as close as possible. Remember your pivot point – if your stern gets too close to the pile, turn towards the pile to pivot your stern away from the danger!

3. Have your crew thread the stern line through the ring as you motor by and gradually pay out the scope. Make sure your fenders are lashed horizontally as vertical hung fenders will roll around the pile and prove useless.

Pile Mooring: The Bow Line

The next stage is to attach the bow line. Have a look at the following figure.

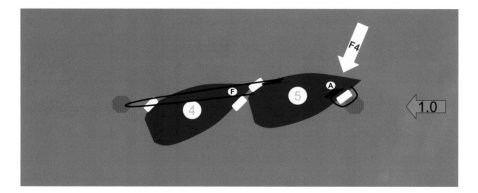

4. Motor upwind of the second pile. Be careful not to get the bow through the wind if possible as the wind will then blow your bow away from the pile, not towards it.

5. Slow down as you approach the second pile. Let the wind blow the fendered area of your starboard bow gently against the pile. Have your crew thread the bow line through the ring and gradually pay out the scope as you start to motor astern.

Pile Mooring: The Finish

Now let's finish up (see figure on the right).

6. Keep paying out the scope of the bow line as you take in the slack on the stern line. When you are equidistant between the piles, tie off as bridles (as shown in the figure) because this helps keep the yacht from swinging out of line with the piles.

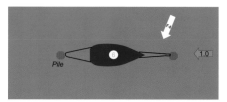

Here are a couple more tips:

- If the tide is in lassoing the piles as you pass by can be very effective.

- If you are staying for a while, replace the slip lines with round turn and two half hitches. Better still, use bow lines with a round turn and ensure the loop of the bow line is very long. This way you can untie

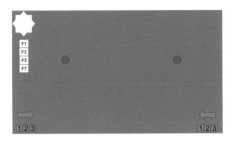

your lines without needing to pull the yacht close to the pile.

PILE MOORING GAME

Have a go at the game on the left, for fun. Get a whiteboard and a dry wipe marker and create the template. Use this to alter wind and tide direction and strength to create some challenging scenarios.

Handling Under Sail

Best practice requires that all skippers are confident in handling under sail.

Fast and efficient sailing is important, so on every journey have the appropriate amount of canvass up and ensure your crew trim the sails effectively throughout.

Later, this chapter provides some exercises so you can practise manoeuvres such as sailing onto a mooring buoy or anchorage and sailing back to a fender thrown overboard.

Before that, however, let's take a look at a few basic points, starting with sail shape and trim.

SAIL SHAPE

Sail trim is a science and an art to which whole books have been devoted. So let's keep it simple. A sail has two basic shape components (see figure on the left):

- chord depth (or draft): this is the fullness of the sail – a greater draft gives a more powerful sail;

- draft position: this affects the entry shape – a forward draft gives a rounder entry, which is more forgiving.

Increase the chord depth if you need extra power in:
- Light winds

- Choppy seas

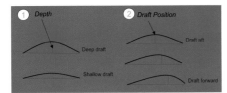

1 Depth Deep draft Shallow draft
2 Draft Position Draft aft Draft forward

Move the draft position aft if you:
- Want good pointing ability

- Have an experienced helm, who can keep the boat pointing in a narrow 'groove'

- Have flat seas

SAIL TWIST

'Twist' is the shape of the sail as you look up the leech. From sail foot to head, the true wind speed increases and its angle becomes freer. This is because the true wind is reduced at the foot due to increased friction with the sea surface.

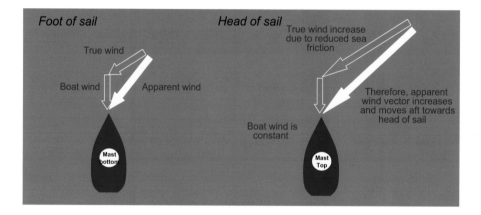

A twisted sail is necessary to maintain the angle of the sail to the apparent wind from head to foot. The manufacturer builds twist into the sail, but you can alter the amount of twist by trimming the sail. Use the telltales on the genoa and main to monitor:
- The entry angle (genoa only)

- The amount of twist

TRIMMING THE GENOA

Sailing upwind, trimming the genoa is very important because:
- its large size makes it your major driving force;

- although it has no mast to disturb the airflow, 'up-wash' from the main creates a freer airflow over the genoa, which 'lifts' the genoa to windward.

1. Adjust entry angle and twist	2. Adjust depth	3. Adjust draft position
How: Sheet & car position	How: Sheet & forestay tension	How: Halyard tension
Symptom: All leeward telltales lift Why: Over-sheeted Action: Ease sheet or head-up	Symptom: Boat speed is reduced in light winds and/or choppy seas	Symptom: Cannot point as high to windward mark as similar yacht
Symptom: All windward telltales lift Why: Under-sheeted Action: Sheet in or bear away	Why: Sail is under powered for conditions	Why: Sail entry not fine enough Action: Loosen halyard
Symptom: Top windward telltale lifts Why: Too much twist Action: Move car forward	Action: Increase depth (draft) by • easing sheet (may have to bear away) • reducing forestay tension (this increases sag in luff and increases draft)	Symptom: Novice helm cannot keep in 'groove' and losing boat speed Why: Sail entry too fine, leads to stalling
Symptom: Lower windward telltale lifts Why: Too little twist Action: Move car aft		Action: Tighten halyard

Always trim your genoa first, as it is the first sail to meet the wind. The disturbed airflow it causes aft affects the mainsail, which should then be trimmed accordingly.

RUDDERLESS SAILING

At this point, we consider the yacht's balance. It is possible to sail the yacht up a river (even tack and gybe) with the wheel locked and it's good fun to try.

Two things affect the yacht's balance:
- net effort around the pivot point of the boat (assume the pivot point on a fin keel boat is around the mast);

- weight distribution.

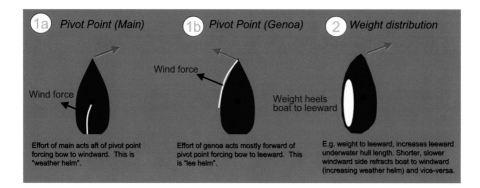

To tack the boat:
1. trim the main;

2. de-power or furl the genoa;

3. move all the weight quickly to leeward.

To gybe the boat:
1. de-power the main;

2. trim the genoa;

3. move all the weight to windward.

TRIMMING THE MAIN

Trimming the main is crucial to good sailing practice. The main sail provides power, but also affects the yacht's helm balance (like the trim tab on a plane):

- A tight leech (little twist) 'kicks' the airflow to windward creating a large heeling force and weather helm.

- A loose leech (lots of twist) allows the air to flow easily off the mainsail, so you feel less weather helm.

About 5–10% weather helm makes for a helm with good feel, without excessive rudder drag.

There are seven main controls for trimming the main – not just the mainsheet! Pay attention to maintaining a well-trimmed main and the journey will be faster and more comfortable.

1. Adjust twist	2. Adjust depth	3. Adjust draft position
How: Mainsheet & Kicker	How: Backstay tension & outhaul	How: Halyard tension & cunningham
Upwind:	Symptom: Heavy airs and/or too much weather helm.	The draft position should normally be 45–50% from the luff, except in light airs when it can be moved back to 55–65%. This is done by easing the halyard tension or cunningham (if the yacht has one).
`Luff up' and check the luff breaks at the same time from foot to head. If it breaks at the head first, there is too much twist so sheet in. If it breaks near the foot first, there is too little twist, so ease the mainsheet.	Why: Sail is over powered for conditions.	
	Action: Decrease depth by	
	• tensioning backstay (flattens top 2/3rd)	
	• tensioning outhaul (flattens bottom 1/3rd)	4. Adjust helm balance
Downwind:	Note: tensioning backstay also moves draft position aft, so tighten halyard accordingly.	How: Traveller position
When bearing away, once the mainsheet is passed the edge of the traveller, the mainsheet cannot keep the boom pulled down to maintain twist. This becomes the function of the kicker.	Symptom: Slow speed in choppy seas	The traveller, NOT the mainsheet, should be used to alter the lead angle of the main sail. As wind strength increases, so the traveller will need to move to leeward. Correct position is determined by the tell-tales and amount of weather helm.
	Why: Sail is under powered for conditions	
	Action: Increase depth by	
	• easing backstay (and halyard)	
	• easing outhaul	

SAILING IN AND OUT OF HARBOUR

Let's take a look at sailing in and out of harbour.

When leaving harbour, raise your sails at the earliest appropriate and safe opportunity. If you are head to wind on the pontoon, why not raise the main while tied up?

When entering harbour, if you're familiar with the harbour or know you will have enough room to drop sail safely in the harbour, sail in.

Remember that the yacht is not at its most manoeuvrable when close tacking or dead running. So if you're concerned about the need to take quick evasive action, have your engine running just in case.

Tip: When close hauled, sail up the windward side of the channel if it's safe. For example, if you are on the starboard side of the channel on port tack, you can neither head up nor bear away! Keeping to port gives you the latter option. Remember: You don't have to pass other motorboats port to port if you are a sailing vessel.

MOORING BUOY: EXERCISE

At some time or another you will have to sail onto a mooring buoy. This provides a good test of your tide and wind awareness and your ability as a skipper. It is straightforward as long as you break it down into five logical steps (A–E as follows).

Mooring Buoy: Sail By
Step A: Approach into tide
Sail past the buoy (on a 'sail by'). Determine the direction of the tide by looking at the buoy's wake or the position of its pick-up buoy. The tide will be your 'brakes', so approach into it.

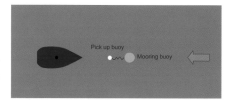

Mooring Buoy: Sail Plan
Step B: Can the main be de-powered?
With the boat into tide, determine the point of sail. Can the main be de-powered? If the wind is abaft the beam, it's unlikely that the main can be released enough to flap (because the shrouds prevent this), but try it. If the main doesn't flap, drop it and approach under genoa.

Here are a couple of tips:
• Using the genoa alone is easier because it's a more forgiving approach and it can be dropped or furled relatively easily.

• Under main, your approach should be on a fine reach: you can de-power the main, but also harden up to be close hauled if necessary.

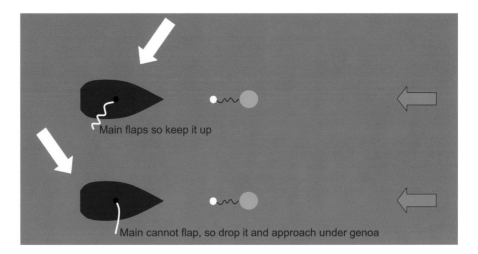

Main flaps so keep it up

Main cannot flap, so drop it and approach under genoa

Mooring Buoy: Right Tack

Step C: Select the tack most into tide

Here, starboard tack puts the yacht across the tide causing two difficulties:

- the tide acts less of a brake;

- the tide will push the yacht downwind with the risk of being headed by the wind.

Choose the tack that puts the yacht more directly into the tide!

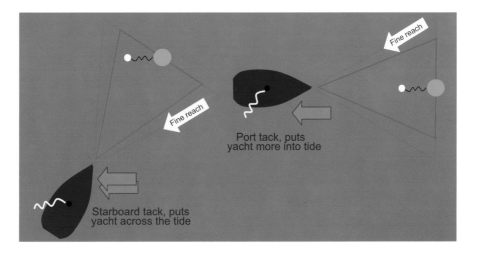

Fine reach

Fine reach

Fine reach

Port tack, puts yacht more into tide

Starboard tack, puts yacht across the tide

Mooring Buoy: Away Reach

Step D: Put your yacht in the right position for the final approach

Position your yacht about six boat lengths from the buoy to give you space to adjust final course and speed.

Under main, when you tack around, the yacht should be a fine reach to the buoy. This requires some careful judgement of wind.

Under main, the yacht should be on a fine reach to the buoy. Under genoa, the point of sail is less important as the sail can be de-powered or furled on any point of sail.

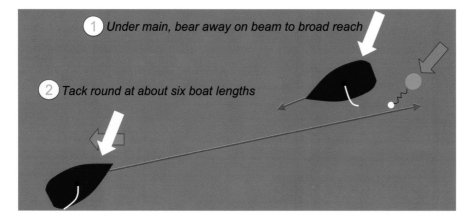

1 Under main, bear away on beam to broad reach

2 Tack round at about six boat lengths

Mooring Buoy: Final Approach

Step E: The final approach

Remember that the buoy is fixed to the sea-bed and unaffected by wind and tide (unlike your yacht). Beware of the tide and/or wind's effect on your yacht. Under main, do not allow the tide to push the yacht too downwind so that you're headed when you tack around.

Pick up the buoy downwind of the buoy. This allows an escape route if you're not successful, i.e. you can bear away from the buoy with no danger of sailing over the mooring chain!

You can use a lasso to catch the buoy, as this gives a wider margin for error than trying a boat hook.

Under main, reduce power further by 'scandalising' (release kicker and hoist topping lift) or back the main.

If you are too fast, don't try and lasso a buoy at 2 knots – be honest, 'bail out' and try again.

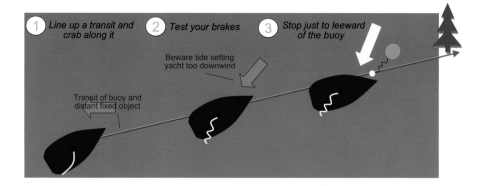

Note that if you ever need to sail onto an anchorage, you can follow the same steps. It's easier in that your target is potentially larger. However, as the final step you must stop and let the tide drift you astern as you lay out the cable. Under main, try and back the main by pushing the boom forward and sailing backwards.

Mooring Buoy Game

Try this game for fun. Get a whiteboard and a dry wipe marker and create the template on the left. Use this to alter wind and tide direction and strength to create some challenging scenarios.

FENDER RETRIEVAL EXERCISE

Best practice requires that a skipper is able to recover a fender under sail.

Note that this is not the same as the procedure for a man over board (MOB) because that is done under power (see Chapter 5). However, the first steps of the fender retrieval procedure are exactly the same as those of the MOB drill.

Fender Retrieval: Crash Tack

The first problem is to stop the boat and establish visual contact with the fender. So 'hove-to' (sometimes called 'crash tack'), i.e. tack without touching the genoa sheets so the genoa is backed.

Point the bows at the fender. The yacht will still sail forward slowly even though the genoa is backed.

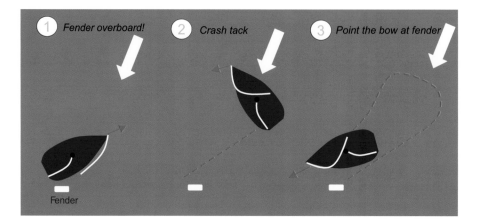

Fender Retrieval: Away Reach

Like sailing onto a mooring buoy, the final approach will be on a fine reach under main alone. Therefore, the key to success is to ensure your away reach puts the yacht in the right position.

Furl the genoa and keep a crew member pointing at the fender! Sail off on a broad reach (120 degrees on your wind instrument). Tack around – the reciprocal of 120 is 60 – for a fine reach!

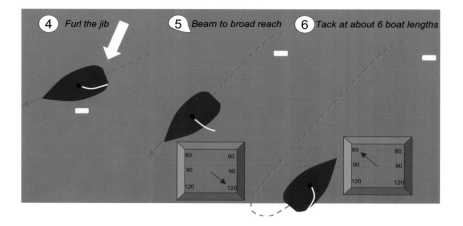

Fender Retrieval: Fill and Spill

Unlike a mooring buoy:

- the fender is also drifting with the tide, so tidal drift can be discounted;

- aim upwind of the fender – it's better to get blown towards it than away because the yacht stops and the bow gets blown away from the wind (see windage in Chapter 3).

If you are on a beam reach and can't spill wind from the main, bear away for a boat length. Point at the fender and try and spill the main again. Repeat as necessary.

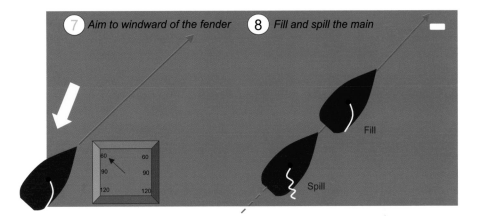

Fender Retrieval: Stop the Yacht

Place a crew member to leeward, forward of the shrouds, with a boat hook. Aim to stop the yacht just upwind of the fender, with no more than 0.5 knots boat speed as the fender reaches your leeward bow.

Beware leeway! In heavy winds, this can set the yacht downwind with the risk of being headed. In this instance, sail away on more of a beam reach so you will tack back onto a beam reach.

To help take the way off the yacht in its final approach, try the following:

- 'scandalise' it – release the kicker and haul up the topping lift;

- back the main – by carefully pushing the boom forward against the wind.

If you're too fast, don't try and pick up the fender at 2 knots – be honest, 'bail out' and try again.

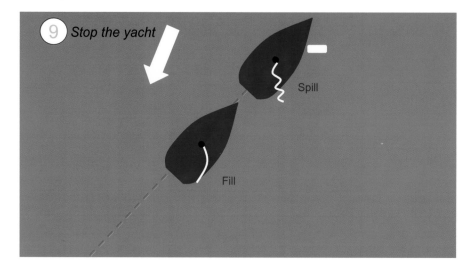

Man Over Board

Best practice demands that all skippers are proficient in picking up a 'man over board' (MOB).

There are many methods of picking up a MOB, but the method described in this chapter works well and is probably the quickest and most repeatable you'll ever try! It can also be done single handed, so if your partner goes overboard you have a sporting chance of recovery.

Remember that MOB is a *power* not a sail manoeuvre. Assuming the very worst happened, and you'd tried unsuccessfully to recover a MOB under sail, a coroner would certainly want to know why you didn't use the engine. You should only sail back to a MOB if you can't start the engine.

STEP A: START THE ENGINE

If you have sufficient crew, carry out the following:

- shout 'man overboard';

- ensure one crew member points at the MOB at all times;

- throw over the Danbuoy immediately to mark the spot;

- press the MOB button on the GPS;

- make a Mayday call. Remember that a crew member has to stay at the VHF – can you afford not to use him or her?

Check for lines in the water, and then start the engine.

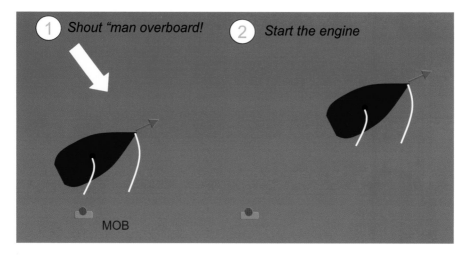

STEP B: CRASH TACK AND HOVE-TO

As with fender recovery (see Chapter 4), the first problem is to stop the boat and keep visual contact with the MOB. So you should 'hove-to' (sometimes called 'crash tack') as follows:

- Tack without touching the genoa sheets (the genoa will be backed).

- Point the bows at the MOB and go hard astern to help stop the yacht dead.

- Turn the wheel full-lock away from the boom. Do this slowly to prevent tacking. Leave helm in that position.

A useful tip is not to crash tack too soon, otherwise you won't have time to stabilise the yacht – tell yourself 'I can do this', and put the helm hard over. However, by the time the engine has been started, it will be time to crash tack.

The yacht should now be hove-to upwind of the MOB with very little or zero yacht speed.

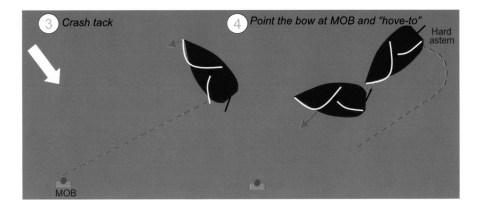

3 Crash tack

4 Point the bow at MOB and "hove-to"

Hard astern

MOB

STEP C: USE THE ENGINE AND LEEWAY

The yacht will drift downwind because of leeway and is generally in a stable position. Use reverse and forward gears to position the yacht directly upwind of the MOB. Be positive when using the power.

Here are a couple of tips to bear in mind:

- If you find that the yacht retains some forward momentum, you need more reverse than forward gear.

- If the bow gets blown down towards the MOB, use a burst of forward gear (the helm is hard over so the bow will move hard to windward).

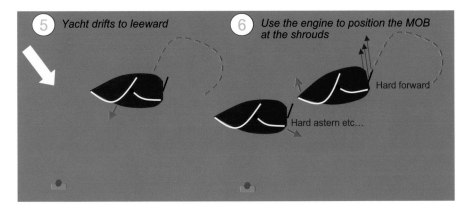

5 Yacht drifts to leeward

6 Use the engine to position the MOB at the shrouds

Hard forward

Hard astern etc...

Remember to ensure that the MOB doesn't come anywhere near the stern, i.e. the propeller. If this happens, engage neutral immediately and revert to the Alternative Method (see page 43).

STEP D: RECOVER THE MOB

Returning to the MOB is the easy part, getting him or her back on board is more difficult, especially if you're on your own. Keep calm – the yacht is stable and protecting the MOB from the wind and waves.

You may have read about many different ways of MOB recovery. The crucial point is to 'keep it simple':

- Get the MOB to the lowest part of the yacht with a boathook, e.g. the stern of a stepped transom.

- Carefully reach down and secure the MOB with one of these two approaches:
  - If the MOB is conscious, tie a large bowline in a line and place under the arms. Attach the other end of the line to a primary winch.

  - If the MOB is unconscious, shackle a spare genoa or spinnaker halyard to the D-ring of the life-vest.

- Winch the MOB onboard and follow the normal First Aid routines as necessary.

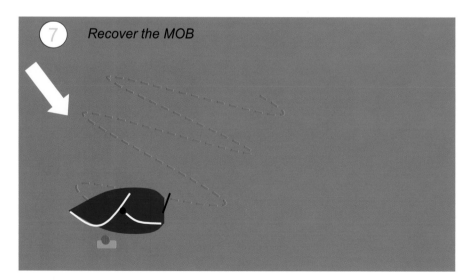

7   *Recover the MOB*

ALTERNATIVE METHOD

The previous MOB method works 95% of the time after a couple of practices, even with novice skippers. However, you may have crash-tacked too soon and the wind may have blown your bow to leeward of the MOB before you could react with a burst of forwards. Don't panic:

- furl or drop the jib, which should be easy to do even if you're shorthanded;

- centre the mainsheet: you won't have time to drop it and centring makes it safe.

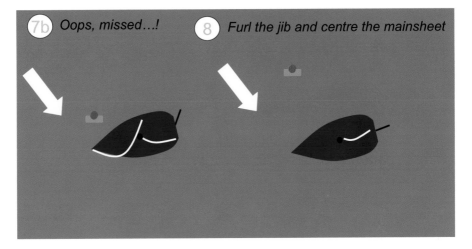

Motor on a broad reach/run away from the MOB to position the yacht about 4 boat lengths downwind.

Tack around and point the bow at the MOB. Here's a tip to help with this manoeuvre:

- Aim just upwind of the MOB to ensure any windage on the bow at low speed blows it towards the MOB.

- Ensure the mainsail can flap; if not, ease the mainsheet.

Stop the boat with the MOB at the leeward shrouds and recover.

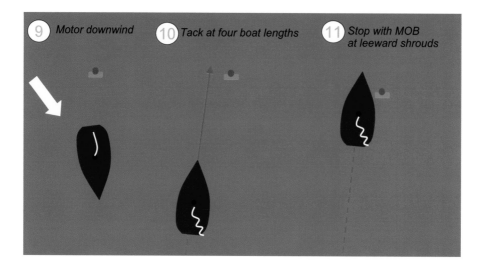

Navigation

A s a skipper, you need to be confident and proficient in navigation, including at night. This chapter contains an exercise in the art of navigation that covers the following best practice requirements. You should aim to get there:

- By the shortest and safest route.

- Efficiently, by using smart navigational techniques.

To allow you to practise your navigation skills and chart work, this chapter also covers two specific drills:

- Navigating in restricted visibility (from the chart table).

- Finding an unlit buoy in the dark.

Allow yourself no more than 30 minutes to prepare your passage plan for this journey.

Assume that you want to sail out of the river Hamble onto a mooring buoy at point C (see figure on page 46).

You have the following relevant information:

- It's 1730 on Friday, 25th November, 2005.

- It's already dark.

- The weather forecast at 1700 stated:
  - wind SW F4–5 veering W
  - rain
  - moderate
  - slight

- The pressure is 1010.
- In these conditions, your fin keel yacht
  - points no more than 40 degrees to the apparent wind
  - tacks through about 90 degrees
  - sails close hauled at about 5 knots.
- Your 12m long yacht has a draft of 1.8m.
- The depth gauge reads from below the keel.
- Variation is 3 degrees West.
- Deviation is zero.

This may look like a simple passage, but with only 30 minutes to plan and get underway, it calls for some mental agility and rough interpolation!

NAVIGATION EXERCISE A: GOOD VISIBILITY

Technique 1: Shortest Safest Route

Draw on the rhumb line. After preparing your pilotage down the Hamble river to a waypoint (say A on the figure), draw on the rhumb line as ground track. The distance is about 3.5M.

Decide whether you can follow it safely. Yes, if you keep a good lookout for ships in the channel; and yes, if there's a 3.4m tide over the shallowest point, Bramble Bank. (1.1 drying + 1.8m draft + 0.5m safety margin = 3.4 required height of tide.)

- At 5 knots you will travel 0.5M in 6 minutes[1]. This passage will take 3.5/0.5 * 6 = 7*6 = about 42 minutes.

4.0		TH	1644	3.7
1.8			2249	2.1
4.1	**25**		0549	3.9
1.9			1142	2.3
4.0		F	1758	3.7
1.7	**26**		0002	2.0
4.2			0657	4.0
1.7		SA	1246	2.1
4.1			1909	3.8
1.4	**27**		0101	1.9
4.5			0751	4.1
1.4		SU	1334	1.9

- Estimated Time of Departure (ETD) at A is 1830. Estimated Time of Arrival (ETA) at Brambles Bank is about 1900. This is HW+1 Portsmouth (3.7m).

  It's close, so you will need to do a quick tidal height calculation later.

---

[1] The 6 minute rule: 6 minutes is 0.1 of an hour, so you will travel 1/10th of your speed in 6 minutes. If your estimated speed is 5 knots, you will travel 0.5M in 6 minutes

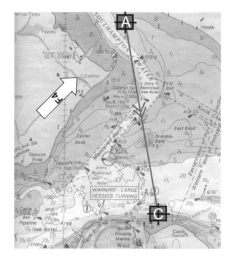

Can you sail the passage on a single tack? Draw on the wind direction. Hopefully, the answer is yes (starboard tack with about 5 degrees leeway on a probable fine reach).

Technique 2: Height of tide (for a Secondary Port)

Use your almanac to calculate the height of tide. The nearest port to the Brambles Bank is Cowes, which is a secondary port of Portsmouth.

			0000	0600	0500	1100			
PORTSMOUTH	50 48N	1 07W	and	and	and	and	4.7	3.8	11
standard port			1200	1800	1700	2300			
Swanage	50 37N	1 57W	−0250	+0105	−0105	−0105	−2.7	−2.3	−4.3
Poole Harbour Entrance	50 41N	1 57W	−0230	+0115	−0045	−0020	−2.5	−2.1	−4.8

Medina River									
Cowes	50 46N	1 18W	−0015	+0015	0000	−0020	−0.5	−0.3	−0.1	0.0
Folly Inn	50 44N	1 17W	−0015	−0015	0000	0000	−0.6			+0.2
Newport	50 42N	1 17W	no data	no data	no data	no data	−0.6	−0.4	+0.1	+0.8

It's roughly neaps as one could discount the 0.1m difference, so HW at Cowes is roughly 3.7m − 0.3m = 3.4m at about 1800 + 0015 = 1815. LW is roughly 2.0m − 0.1m = 1.9m, so the range is 3.4 − 1.9 = 1.5m.

1900 is HW+1. Using the rule of twelfths[2], it will fall 1/12th of its range = 0.13m (for a falling tide, let us call it 0.2m to be safe).

4.0		TH 1644	3.7
1.8		2249	2.1
4.1	25	0549	3.9
1.9			
4.0		F 1758	3.7
1.7	26	0002	2.0
4.2			
1.7		SA 1246	2.1
4.1		1909	3.8
1.4	27	0101	1.9
4.5		0751	4.1
1.4		SU 1334	1.9

You will only have a 3.2m tide (0.3m under the keel) on a falling tide. But its low barometric pressure with a slight sea and you'll be heeled over. What would you do?

Technique 3: Pilotage

Draw a rolling road. You decide not to risk Brambles Bank, so you'll need some simple pilotage to avoid it. One option is to sail down clearing transits leaving three green channel markers just to port.

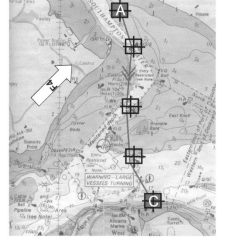

Draw a rough 'rolling road' and put in a waterproof wallet to keep with you in the cockpit so as to avoid being at the chart table.

---

[2] The rule of twelfths: the fall of tide over about 6 hours can be approximated to 1/12th in the first hour, 2 1/12ths in the second, 3 1/12ths in the third etc... 1:2:3:3:2:1

A good tip is to keep distances between waypoints appropriate to visibility at night.

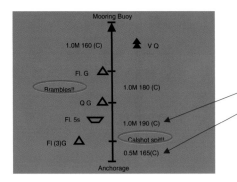

Note: These are compass bearings to waypoints so the crew know what to look out for. They are not courses to steer!

Technique 4: Course to Steer

Draw a course to steer to account for tidal effect. This modified route should raise a question in your mind. The dog-leg with a course over ground (COG) of 187 degrees is close to the true wind at 225 degrees. Can you sail that COG on that leg?

Look at the Solent tidal atlas for Portsmouth HW+1 (below):

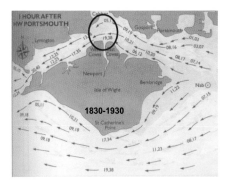

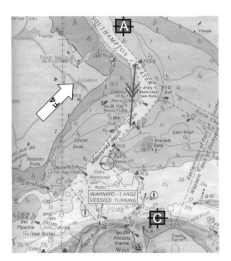

To get a quick course to steer, you don't have to work in real NM. Simply use the same units for both tide and boat speed vectors and the trigonometry works! Use units on the Breton plotter, for example (inches or cm).

Plot your true COG at 187 and 0.5M (0.5cm) tide setting 225. Mark off your speed of 5 knots (5cm). This gives you a rough CTS of due south.

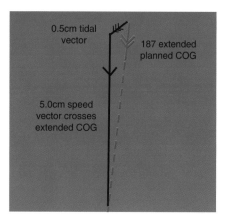

0.5cm tidal vector

187 extended planned COG

5.0cm speed vector crosses extended COG

Remember to add leeway (say 5 degrees) and variation west (3 degrees).

A CTS of 190 (C) is only 35 degrees off true wind. Remember that your 5 knot boat wind will bring the apparent wind further forward. So, unless the wind veers, expect to tack for the QG mark!

Technique 5: Lee Bow

Select the more desirable tack. Suppose that when you arrive at position B in the figure on the left, the wind suddenly backs and it starts to rain. At this point there'll be between 0.5 and 1.9 knots of tide setting about west-southwest.

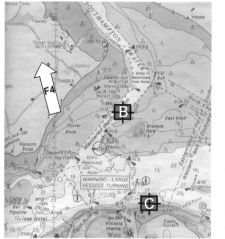

Your destination C is now directly into wind! You're headed, but which is your preferred tack?

The answer is starboard tack: You'll have the tide setting towards the lee of your bow. This is called 'lee-bow-ing' the tide – it's a classic racing strategy for getting to a windward mark. You may not be a racing skipper, but of course sailing efficiently is part of good practice. Let's look at the principle of lee-bowing in more detail.

Lee-bowing is caused by the effect the tide has on the apparent wind. You could interpolate a figure of 1.5 knots of tide. This will cause you to feel a 1.5 knot 'tide wind' in the opposite direction. The result of true and tide winds is a 'sailing wind' vector, i.e. the apparent wind if your yacht was not sailing forwards. In this example, the tide wind creates a veer of the sailing wind, thus 'lifting' the yacht on starboard tack up to the windward mark C by about 4 degrees.

Remember that this tactic also leaves you up-tide of your ultimate destination, which is desirable.

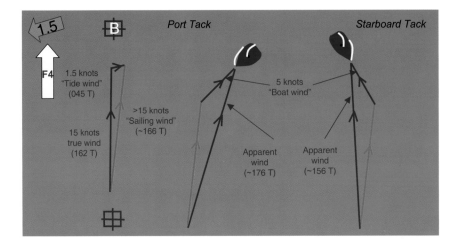

Technique 6: Reverse Vectors

Decide the optimum place to tack. You are now on starboard tack and know you will have to tack to approach the mooring buoy at C (see figure on the right). However, remember that:

- if you tack too soon, you must tack again;

- if you tack too late, you'll travel further than necessary.

Choosing the correct place to tack is crucial to arriving at your destination as efficiently as possible. When should you tack?

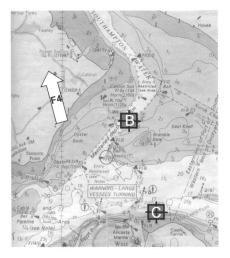

You note your current bearing on starboard tack is 119 (M). You know your yacht will tack through 90 degrees, so your bearing on the next tack will be about 209 (M) or 206 (T). You need to predict the COG on your next tack. When point C is on a bearing equal to your predicted COG, tack! This is called a 'reverse vector'.

Remember that there's no reason not to use electronic navigational aids, i.e. GPS.

Using the cm scale on your Breton plotter, draw on the speed and tidal vectors (as though you were doing a future EP). Add leeway and measure the future COG – 216 (T). When point C bears 216 (T) – if you have entered it as a waypoint on GPS – or 219 (M) on your handheld compass, tack!

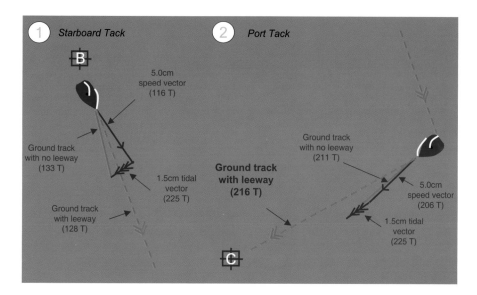

Technique 7: Velocity Made Good (VMG)

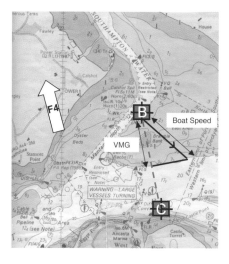

Try to maximise your Velocity Made Good (VMG). This is your actual speed over the ground in the direction of your mark. You can use your GPS to monitor Velocity Made Good (VMG). VMG upwind or downwind is a compromise between pointing ability and boat speed:

• if you point directly to C, your boat speed may fall;

• if you bear away to increase your boat speed, you travel less directly to C.

Make single alterations to the sail trim and allow the helm to settle to that new trim. If the VMG increases it was a good alteration. Otherwise, revert and try something else!

Here's a good tip: Don't ask the helm to steer to VMG – the temptation will be to pinch and see a momentary increase in VMG. This results in a stalled genoa and a yacht that then slows down too much! Remember that when sailing upwind, the helm should only be sailing to the genoa telltales:

- If the windward telltales lift, bear away until they fly back.

- If the leeward telltales lift, head up until they fly back.

As the true wind increases, your optimum angle to that true wind, as a rule, decreases upwind and increases downwind.

NAVIGATION EXERCISE B: BLIND NAVIGATION

Blind navigation is a good way of practising your navigational skills and chart work, so that you're prepared for those times when you need to navigate the boat from the chart table only and when electronic navigational aids can't be used.

For this exercise, you have four main navigational aids:

- depth gauge;

- speed and trip (log);

- course steered by the helm;

- communication with the crew.

Therefore, before starting you must confirm the following:

- your speed/trip is working accurately;

- your yacht's draft;

- the point on the yacht from which your depth gauge reads;

- a modus operandi with your crew for communication between chart table and cockpit.

Let's assume it's now later that evening. You plan to sail off the mooring buoy at Cowes, head west and anchor for supper in Newtown river. At 2000, you're on your way. The wind has veered west and it's drizzling.

As you tack past Egypt point, visibility drops to a cable (1ca). You have to go below and navigate the yacht to

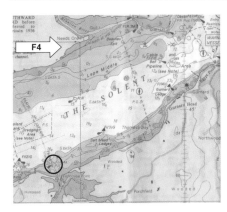

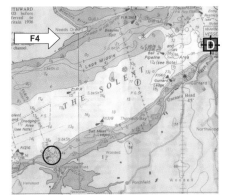

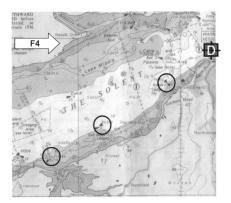

the red buoy (Fl.R.4s) at the mouth of Newtown river (see figure on the left). Here's what to do.

Step 1: Fix Position

Fix your position and stop. If you're unable to use GPS, use nearby lit buoys. Here are a couple of tips:

- If it's safe to do so, hove-to.

- Better still, if visibility allows, ask your crew to sail to the closest buoy (the nearby north cardinal) and remain there to await further instructions. This can buy you time to think.

Let's assume you are at the north cardinal.

Step 2: Plan Passage

Break the passage up into smaller manageable legs, by having interim waypoints.

The two navigational methods you will then use are:

A: buoy hopping (course to steer)

B: follow a contour

Remember that for an accurate course to steer, your actual and planned speed through the water must be equal. Accurate helming to a compass bearing is also key. This is easier to achieve under motor. Furthermore, the westerly wind (270 T) means you would have to tack, adding a huge level of complexity you can well do without.

Let's assume that, in this case, you can start the engine and drop the sails.

Method A: Buoy Hop

The red buoy is 4.5M away and visibility is only 0.1NM. Using the '1 in 60 rule' [3], a normal 5 degree navigational or helming error over this distance would mean you pass 0.4NM away. You would probably miss it!

---

[3] The 1 in 60 rule: using the link between degrees and NM, a 1 degree error over a 60NM passage will pass 1NM from your destination. Basic trigonometry says a 5 degree error over 6NM will pass 0.5 NM away.

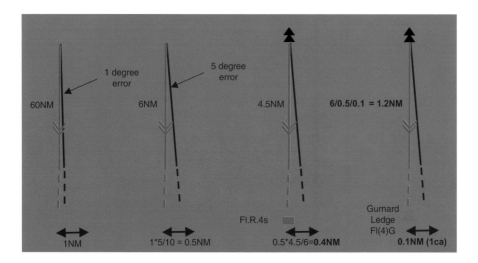

So, in 1ca visibility with a 5 degree error margin, aim to find interim waypoints that are no more than 6 / 0.5/0.1 = 1.2NM apart, e.g. 'Gurnard Ledge' starboard mark. Any interim achievement will also provide a confidence boost.

Method B: Follow Contour

In this case, the 'Salt Mead' starboard mark is almost 2NM from 'Gurnard Ledge' (E), so a course to steer is likely to fail (see figure on the right).

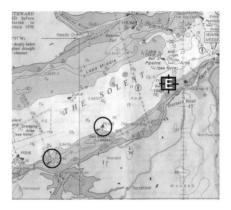

However, like many other buoys, this is on or near a contour line. It is 1ca north of the 10m contour. Follow just north of the 10m contour and you are likely to pass very close.

Always ensure you find the contour line up-tide of the target buoy so as not to risk passing it before you find the contour. In this case, aim south from Gurnard Ledge.

Similarly, the red buoy is too far away for a course to steer. So head south and pick up and follow the 5m contour on which it lies.

Step 3: Prepare to Estimate Position

To start navigating, you'll need Estimated Positions (EP) and the ability to find contour lines. A good EP

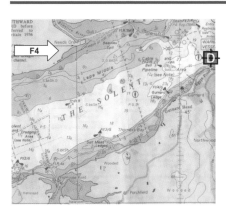

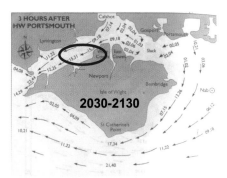

2030-2130

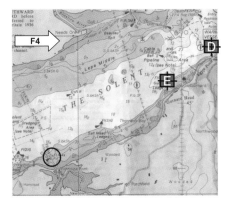

confirmed by a depth reading is the best way to fix your position. Therefore, you'll need to determine respectively:

- Tidal stream

- Tidal height

You estimate the passage will occur between 2030 and 2130 (HW+3). It's roughly neaps and 1.5 knots with you.

Use Cowes as the secondary port (you already have that information). The range is 1.5m and by the end of the third hour it will have fallen half its range. This gives a tidal height of about 2.7m (3.4 – 0.7).

Step 4: Navigate

Once you are ready, brief your crew thoroughly and start your passage.

Reset the trip to zero (0.0) and note the exact time (or start your stop watch).

Find 'Gurnard Ledge' (E) (see figure on the left) and then do the following:

- Ask your helm to steer 240 (M) at exactly 5 knots. It is 1.2NM away. Your COG should be roughly identical. Your Speed Over Ground (SOG) – with the following tide – will be 6.5 knots.

- Using the 6 minute rule, in 6 minutes your yacht will travel 0.65NM and 1.3NM in 12 minutes. Look for the buoy in about 10 minutes!

- At the buoy, stop the yacht, make a log entry and plot your position on the chart.

If mental arithmetic is not your strong point, remember that your Almanac contains a 'Speed, time and distance' table. This tells you how long it will take you (minutes) to travel any distance (NM) at any given SOG (knots).

Next, find the 10m contour line:

- Ask your helm to motor due south at say 3.5 knots (finding and following a contour line can be easier at reduced speed).

- Ask one crew member to monitor the depth gauge until it reads 10.9m (10.0 + 2.7 − 1.8m), at which point you'll be over the 10m contour.

Now, find 'Salt Mead' (F, see figure):

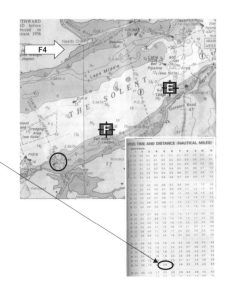

- Ask the helm to steer to starboard and keep to 10.9m. If the depth increases, steer to port and vice-versa.

- It is about 2NM away and, at 5.0 knots SOG, this will take about 20 minutes.

- Ask a crew member to monitor the course steered and watch for a dog-leg to starboard from 240 (M) to about 285 (M). When this happens, you are only about 4 minutes away.

- You might ask the helm to keep to slightly deeper water, say 12.9m, as 'Salt Mead' is deeper than the 10m contour!

- At the buoy, stop the yacht, make a log entry and plot your position on the chart.

You can now find your red buoy as above by following the 5m contour line.

If you need to sail, you'll have to short tack between 2 contour lines.

Remember that the length of your tacks must reduce as visibility reduces, to avoid the risk of sailing further away from the buoy than the visibility. For example, tacking between the 10m contour (10.9m) and 2m contour (2.9m), should take you close enough to the red buoy.

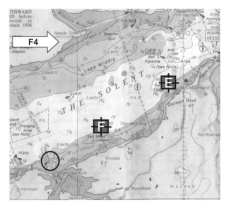

This method is less likely to succeed for the two starboard marks as there's no well-defined 15m contour to starboard! Tack on the 10m (10.9). Watch the trip on port tack until the depth gauge reads 12.9m. If you travel more than say 2ca, reduce your tacking depth to 11.9m.

Tip: If in doubt, shorten the tacks – at least it will keep your crew warm!

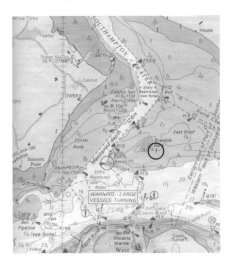

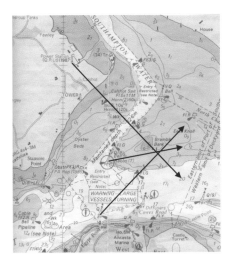

NAVIGATION EXERCISE C: FINDING UNLIT MARKS IN THE DARK

Finding unlit marks in the dark is a relatively simple drill that is very useful for testing best practice of your navigational skills and chart work. In this exercise, you set a destination, but this time you won't be confined to the chart table. Communication with the cockpit shouldn't be an issue and you should be able to see lit buoys and landmarks at their normal visible range for the conditions.

You need to be well-prepared. Along with a powerful torch, your four main navigational aids are:

- hand bearing compass that can be illuminated at night;
- depth gauge;
- speed and trip (log);
- course steered by the helm.

Let's assume it's after tea. Instead of heading west to Newtown, you decide to sail off the mooring buoy at Cowes by 2030 and find the unlit Brambles Bank post. You have already calculated height of tide as 2.7m.

There is always more than one way to solve a navigational problem. How many different ways can you think of in this case?

The trick is to find the most suitable solution for the situation – the one most likely to succeed that can also be worked out reasonably quickly. Let's look at some possible solutions.

Technique 1: Two transits. Sail down a back transit of the north cardinal and FL.G starboard mark, until the Fawley power station chimney and Q.G starboard mark come into transit.

Technique 2: Transit and bearing. Sail down a back transit of the north cardinal and Fl.G starboard mark, until the west cardinal bears 260 (M).

Now let's assume we have only two lit marks: the nearby north cardinal and Fl.G starboard mark.

Technique 3: Back bearing and depth. Sail to the Fl.G starboard mark. Then sail away on a back bearing of 223 (M). At the 2m contour the depth gauge will read 2.9m (2.0 + 2.7 – 1.8m). Keep a look out with the torch as the depth drops.

Technique 4: Back bearing and distance run. Sail to the Fl.G starboard mark and stay there. Calculate your SOG as being 4.4 knots:

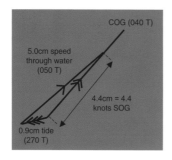

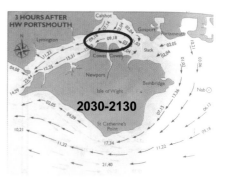

1NM over the ground = 1.14 NM (5/4.4) on trip. The distance to the post is 0.55NM, so on arrival the trip will read 0.77NM (0.55 * 1.14). Reset your trip to 0.0. Sail away on a back bearing of 223 (M) and watch the trip. When the trip approaches your target reading, look out!

Technique 5: Course to steer and distance run. As per Solution 4, but instead of maintaining a back bearing, ask the helm to steer 048 (M) – assuming 5 degrees leeway under sail. Remember that your crew must keep the boat speed at 5.0 knots. Clearly, this is easier under motor than sail.

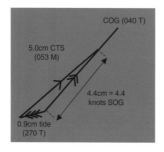

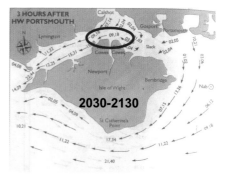

What other methods or combinations did you find? Which method did you prefer and why?

Passage Planning

A s a skipper, best practice demands that you're able to plan and skipper all sorts of offshore passages. This chapter contains a comprehensive exercise in the art of passage planning.

PASSAGE PLANNING: EXERCISE
Let's say that you need to plan a passage as follows:
- Passage: 'Hamble to St Vaast'.

- Depart: 'after lunch some time on Friday, 25 November, 2005'.

- Weather for Wight: 'SW backing south 4–5, fair, good, moderate'.

It should take about 90 minutes to complete the plan. You need to be methodical and keep to the right level of detail.

Note that this exercise is a test of your passage planning, so you're not expected to complete detailed pilotage plans out of the river Hamble, for example.

Passage Planning Checklist
On page 60 is a checklist to help you manage your planning time more effectively.

The exact time for each step will differ depending on the nature of your passage and the different complexities of each step. You will need a full tank of fuel and must ensure you have enough of the right food and drink for the journey.

Step A: What is the total distance?

(Remember: Always start with the chart covering both departure and destination ports.)

The distance is about 85NM via the eastern Solent and about 90 via the Needles.

Step B: What is the weather forecast?

The wind force is F4–5, so you should be able to make 5 knots boat speed under full canvass. It should be a pleasant sail!

Step C: How long will it take?

At 5 knots estimated boat speed, the passage will take 17–18 hours depending on which route you follow to leave the Solent.

Draw the wind directions on the chart to the right. Are you able to sail a direct route with a SW wind?

If the wind backs south you'll have to beat. Your VMG may then drop by a 1/3rd or more! Let's assume for now that the wind remains SW.

Which way would you leave the Solent? Leaving via the west:

- would be a beat into wind;

- adds distance;

- goes through a tidal gate at the Needles;

- but provides a favourable cross-channel wind angle!

Step	Description	Time to go (min)	Suggested Time (min)
A	Total distance	90	5
B	Weather forecast	85	5
C	Journey time	80	5
D	Time windows	75	15
E	Tidal gates	60	15
F	Course to steer	45	15
G	Wind strategy	30	10
H	Hazards	20	10
I	Ports of refuge	10	5
J	Watch system	5	5
K	Victualling		

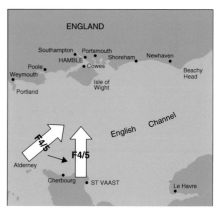

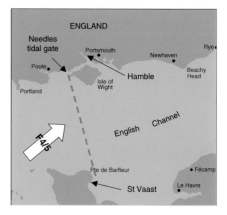

ST VAAST-LA-HOUGUE 9.22.9

Manche 49°35'·19N 01°15'·43W ⚓⚓⚓⚓☆☆☆

CHARTS AC 1349, *2135, 2613*; SHOM 7090, 6864, 7056, 7120; ECM 527, 528; Imray C32; Stanfords 1, 7, 21

TIDES –0240 Dover; ML 4·1; Duration 0530; Zone –0100
Standard Port CHERBOURG (←—)

Times				Height (metres)			
High Water		Low Water		MHWS	MHWN	MLWN	MLWS
0300	1000	0400	1000	6·4	5·0	2·5	1·1
1500	2200	1600	2200				
Differences ST VAAST-LA-HOUGUE							
+0120	+0050	+0120	+0115	+0·3	+0·5	0·0	–0·1

SHELTER Excellent in marina, 2·3m; lock open HW–2¼ to HW+3. Crowded in season. If full, ⚓ awaiting lock, ⚓ off in White sector of jetty It between brgs of 330° and 350°, but this becomes untenable in strong E–S winds.

NAVIGATION WPT 49°34'·34N 01°13'·86W, 130°/310° from/to main jetty It (Oc 6s) 1·3M. Appr in W sector, leaving le Gavendest SCM By to stbd and Le Bout du Roc ECM By and Le Creux de Bas ECM bn to port. The ent is wide and well marked. Beware boats at ⚓, cross currents and oyster beds. "Le Run" appr is not advised and should not be attempted >1·2m draft.

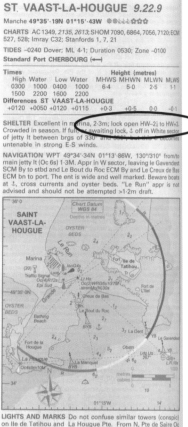

LIGHTS AND MARKS Do not confuse similar towers (conspic) on Ile de Tatihou and La Hougue Pte. From N, Pte de Saire Oc (2+1) 10s 11m 10M. From E, ldg lts 267·3°: front La Hougue Oc 4s 9m 10M; rear Morsalines Oc (4) WRG 12s 90m 11/8M in W sector. Main jetty hd lt, Oc (2) WRG 6s 12m 10/7M, W tr + R top, vis W310°-350°. R/G tfc sigs at lock ent.

RADIO TELEPHONE VHF Ch 09.

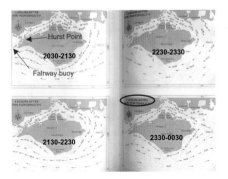

Step D: Are there time limits?

You can depart Hamble at any time. However, you may have never been to St Vaast. Read the Almanac well as all it contains all the information. The marina maintains 2.3m[1] and a lock gate opens HW–2¼ to HW+3. The standard port is Cherbourg:

Time is short. The second high water looks more achievable. Use mental interpolation to calculate the second HW. The time range:

- is 30 min (+0120 minus +0050);

- occurs over 7 hours (2200 minus 1500);

- over 1 hour is 30/7 = about 4 1/2 min;

- in about 2 hours (1650 minus 1500) is about 4*2 .5 = about 9 mins.

HW St Vaast is +0120 – 9 = +0111 min = roughly 1800 FST (1700 UT).

You need to arrive between 1445 and 2000 UT on Saturday. What time would you depart Hamble?

Step E: Are there any tidal gates to plan for?

You plan to arrive early, because it will be daylight and there is a contingency for possible delays. Your planned departure time is 2045 (1445 – 18 hours).

---

[1] The entrance dries, but the Almanac doesn't indicate to what height. Can you assume 2.3m of water in the entrance when the lock gates are open? To be sure, find the most detailed chart and check detailed drying heights and height of tide needed!

You decide to leave via the west to have the favourable cross-channel wind-angle.

Hurst point is 14NM and the fairway buoy a further 4NM. Can you get through the Needles before the tide turns and floods at 2330?

You decide, 'No': You could set off earlier, but don't want to start a long journey with a beat to windward with wind against tide. So you plan to leave via the east and risk the wind being freer when you get out of the Solent.

Step F: What is your cross-channel CTS

You plan a nice reach down the eastern Solent and aim to arrive at W. Princessa buoy at about 2330. You need a quick CTS. This can take a long time, so here's a quick method:

1. Mark up a cross-channel tidal stream atlas. The reference port for this atlas is Dover and it's a below average range neap.

2. Draw on your rhumb line from W. Princessa to a point where the E–W tidal flow stops, say Pointe de Barfluer. This rhumb line is 185 (T).

3. On the edge of a piece of paper, mark off the two waypoints as shown in the top figure on the right. Use the scale on the tidal atlas to measure the cross channel distance. Here, it's about 1 degree or 60NM.

4. This cross-channel element will take 12 hours at 5 knots boat speed. So divide the scale into 12 equal hourly units. Create a table for West and East going tide as shown in the figure on the right.

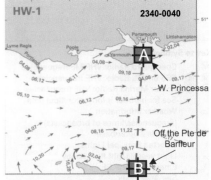

I Hour before HW Dover (0130 before HW Portsmouth)

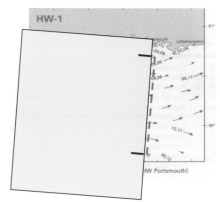

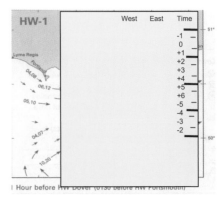

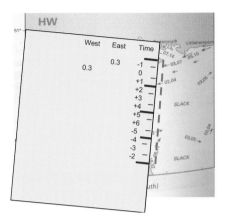

West	East	Time	
	0.3	-1	
0.3		0	
1.3		+1	
1.4		+2	
1.9		+3	
1.5		+4	
1.2		+5	
	slack	+6	
	1.5	-5	
	2.5	-4	
	2.8	-3	
	2.3	-2	
7.6	9.4		
	1.8 net East		

5. Read the neap rate and set nearest the first hour (on the HW-1 tidal atlas) – 0.3 knots east. Then read the neap rate and set nearest the second hour (HW tidal atlas) – 0.3 knots west.

6. Continue for the full twelve hour crossing, until we have a net tidal set[2].

You will arrive at Pointe De Barfleur with a couple of hours of favourable tide down the coast towards St Vaast!

7. The 1 in 60 rule tells us that a 1 degree error over 60NM gives a 1NM offset. So your 1.8NM east offset equates to an almost 2 degree net course correction west.

8. Your CTS is 195(M): (185(T) + 2 course correction west + 3 variation + 5 leeway).

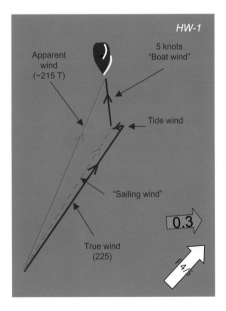

_____

[2] Note the stronger tidal rates nearer the French coast.

If the true wind angle is indeed SW 225(T), can you sail that course? A quick guess would say 'No', and you also know that:
– the boat wind will move the apparent wind forward;

– you're not lee-bowing in the first hour, so this will also move the apparent wind forward.

You won't have time to work this out, nor would you want to! You decide to stay with your plan and see what the actual wind conditions are when you arrive.

You arrive at W. Princessa on time. The apparent wind is 215(T). Your best course is 178(M).

Step G: What is your wind strategy?

On this course you'll arrive about 17NM east of your waypoint at Pointe de Barfleur: 195(M) – 178(M) = 17 degrees off course over 60NM. So you'll have to tack onto port for a few hours, but the question is when?

To lee-bow the tide and get lifted more to the windward waypoint, you should be on:
• port tack when the tide sets east;

• starboard tack when the tide sets west.

However, the wind is forecast to back south. What's your wind strategy? Here are a couple of tips:
• 'Sail towards the expected wind shift'. In this case, starboard sails you towards the expected wind back. Normally you would tack on the wind shift when you're headed. However, to take advantage of lee-bowing, it may pay to wait until the tide starts to flood east at 0730.

• If the wind backs before 0730 and you're in doubt, enter the waypoint into GPS to see which tack maximises your VMG.

Cross Channel Game

Get a whiteboard and a dry wipe marker and create the template on the right. Use this to alter wind and net tide

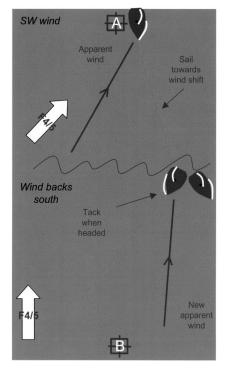

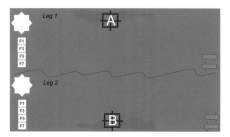

direction and strength for legs 1 and 2 of a cross chan-nel passage. Create some challenging cross-channel scenarios. Have fun!

Step H: What hazards must you avoid or be aware of?

Keep a good look out for ships when crossing the two shipping lanes. The east–west lane is 20NM from W. Princessa. You'll arrive there at about 0330 and it will take about an hour to cross.

As skipper, you should be on deck at these times.

Ensure your radar reflector is in place (your tiny tricol-our won't be readily visible to large ships!).

This is not a TSS, but choosing to tack onto port and sailing along the shipping lanes wouldn't be safe.

Step I: What are your ports of refuge?

Remember that a good port of refuge must be acces-sible 24 hours in any conditions. Read the Almanac thoroughly to ensure this is the case. Here, Portsmouth or Cherbourg fit this requirement.

Step J: What watch system will you use?

Assume you have a crew of four, including you as skip-per.

There are many ways to organise a watch system, but consider your crew and the conditions. It's very much more tiring to stand watch on a cold night in rough seas than during a warm day in slight seas.

Two sets of eyes are better than one, especially at night: one crew can steer while the second navigates or prepares food.

You must keep your crew fed and warm, so plan who prepares food and when.

Discuss the pros and cons of the three possible watch systems opposite. Create a watch system to suit you and your crew.

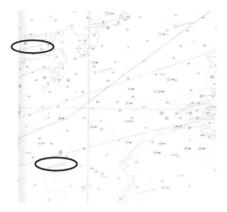

'2 on-2 off' 3 hour

Time	On	On	Off	Off
1130–0100	Skip	A	B	C
0100–0230	B	C	Skip	A
0230–0400	Skip	A	B	C
0400–0530	B	C	Skip	A

Rolling 1 hour

Time	On (Helm)	On (Nav)	Off	Off
1130–0030	Skip	A	B	C
0030–0130	C	Skip	A	B
0130–0230	B	C	Skip	A
0230–0330	A	B	B	Skip
0330–0430	Skip	A	B	C

Rolling 1.5 hour

Time	On (Helm)	On (Nav)	Off	Off
1130–0100	B	C	Skip	A
0100–0230	A	B	C	Skip
0230–0400	Skip	A	B	C
0400–0530	C	Skip	A	B
0530–0700	B	C	Skip	A

And finally, What-If scenarios

Now that you've spent time developing your passage plan, it's a good exercise to think about some 'what if' scenarios. The sort of events you may like to consider can include the following:

- You run into advection fog as you approach the first east–west shipping lane.

- You run into a bank of radiation fog 5 miles off the Cherbourg peninsular.

- The southerly wind increases F6 half way across the channel with a falling barometer.